D1716874

National Day Traditions around the World

by Susan Kesselring • illustrated by Elisa Chavarri

The Child's World

Published by The Child's World®
1980 Lookout Drive • Mankato, MN 56003-1705
800-599-READ • www.childsworld.com

Acknowledgments
The Child's World®: Mary Berendes, Publishing Director
Red Line Editorial: Editorial direction
The Design Lab: Design
Amnet: Production

Design elements: Shutterstock Images

Photographs ©: Monkey Business Images/Shutterstock Images, Cover,
Title; Kudryashka/Shutterstock Images, 5; David P. Lewis/iStockphoto, 7;
Shutterstock Images, 13, 27; Bartlomiej Magierowski/Shutterstock
Images, 17; Migel/Shutterstock Images, 21; Igor Karon/iStockphoto, 25;
Elaine Willcock/Shutterstock Images, 29

ISBN 9781614734284
LCCN 2012946513

Printed in the United States of America
Mankato, MN
November, 2012
PA02145

About the Author

Susan Kesselring is a K-1 teacher, writer of children's books, and mother of five adult daughters. She lives in Minnesota with her husband, Rob, and crazy dog, Lois Lane. She loves kids, books, music and nature.

About the Illustrator

Elisa Chavarri is a Peruvian illustrator who works from her home in Alpena, Michigan, which she shares with her husband, Matt, and her cat, Sergeant Tibbs. She has previously illustrated *Fly Blanky Fly*, by Anne Margaret Lewis, and *Fairly Fairy Tales*, by Esmé Raji Codell.

Table of Contents

Chapter One

What Are National Days?

Since early times, countries have tried to rule other countries. Sometimes, one country takes over another country through war. Sometimes a country agrees to let another country rule it.

But often, the country being ruled wants to be free. The people want to make their own rules. They may even fight for freedom.

When a country becomes independent, the people often create a National Day. Sometimes they call this their **Independence** Day. On this day, the people of a country **celebrate** their freedom together. They remember all the good things about their country.

People stay home from work and school. They gather with family and friends and eat special foods. Many countries have parades, concerts, and fireworks. The people fly their country's flag and sing their national **anthem**, or song. They may dress up in special clothes or wear the colors of the flag.

People enjoy their National Day. It is a time to be proud of their country.

*People around the world watch fireworks
on their National Days.*

Chapter Two

Canada Day

Great Britain ruled Canada until July 1, 1867. On that day, Canada became an independent country. Today, the people still celebrate their independence on July 1. The day was first called Dominion Day. In 1983, it was given a new name: Canada Day.

Today, people celebrate Canada Day with parades. The Royal Canadian Mounted Police, or Mounties, ride their horses in the parades. They wear their bright red uniforms.

People go to carnivals, festivals, and sporting events. They have barbecues outdoors. The red and white Canadian flag flies everywhere. Some people paint their faces red and white. They wear red and white clothes to match the flag. At night they watch fireworks. They sing Canada's national anthem, "O Canada."

People celebrate Canada Day in Ottawa, the capital city.

In Kenya, people celebrate *Jamhuri* (jahm-HOO-ree) Day on December 12. Jamhuri means **"republic"** in Swahili. Swahili is one language spoken in Kenya. Kenya became its own country on December 12, 1964. The United Kingdom ruled Kenya before that day.

On Jamhuri Day, people dance, sing, and march in parades. They listen to their leaders give speeches. The leaders talk about what makes Kenya great and about making Kenya even better in the future.

Many people travel back to their home villages. They want to be with family on this special day. They cook together. They eat delicious foods like *nyama choma* (nyah-mah CHOH-mah), which is roasted goat meat.

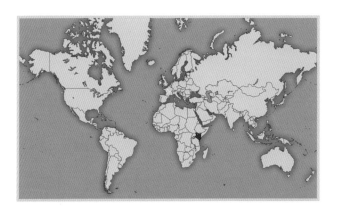

Chapter Four

El Grito de Dolores

Many people think Mexico's Independence Day is *Cinco de Mayo* (SEEN-koh day MEYE-oh), or May 5. But it's not! Cinco de Mayo celebrates one battle in Mexico's war with France. Mexico's Independence Day is *El Grito de Dolores* (el GREE-toh day do-LOH-res) on September 16.

Spain ruled Mexico for hundreds of years. By the 1800s, the Mexican people wanted freedom. Then, something happened early in the morning on September 16, 1810. In the tiny town of Dolores, a priest named Father Hidalgo (ee-DAHL-go) rang the church bells. He gave a *grito*, or cry, for independence. He told the people to fight to make their country free. This was the start of a long fight. When it ended in 1821, Mexico was a free country.

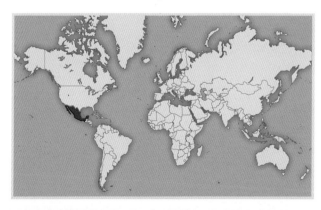

Today, people celebrate El Grito de Dolores, or "the Cry of Dolores," all over Mexico. It begins at 11:00 p.m. on September 15. Mexico's president appears on the balcony of the National Palace. Crowds of people come to watch. He cries out, "*¡Viva México! ¡Viva la independencia!*" This means, "Long live Mexico! Long live independence!" The crowd echoes back his cry.

All over the country, leaders of states and towns do the same. People throw confetti. They watch red, green, and white fireworks. These are the colors of the Mexican flag.

The next day is El Grito de Dolores. On September 16, people don't have to go to work or school. They celebrate all day with fiestas, bullfights, rodeos, and parades. They are proud of their free country.

Mexicans march in parades on El Grito de Dolores.

Chapter Five

Finnish Independence Day

Finland became independent from Russia on December 6, 1917. Russia had ruled Finland for more than 100 years. Finnish people celebrate each year on this date.

Each family lights two candles in their home. The candles are blue and white like the Finnish flag. When Russia ruled Finland, people put blue and white candles in their windows. This showed that they wanted Finland to be free from Russia. Now they light the candles on Independence Day to remember that time.

People watch a military parade. Students march to the graves of soldiers. The leader of the country holds a fancy dinner and dance for 2,000 people. This is shown on television. Many people also watch a favorite movie, *The Unknown Soldier*, on television.

Chapter Six

National Day of the People's Republic of China

The People's Republic of China formed on October 1, 1949. People all over China celebrate October 1 as the National Day of the People's Republic of China. People have a whole week off work and school. This is called "Golden Week." During this week, Chinese people travel and visit famous places in their country.

The Chinese flag is raised in the capital city of Beijing. The flag is red with yellow stars. People may go to the National Day parade to see colorful floats. There are people in costumes from different parts of China. Many soldiers march. They have practiced so they move at exactly the same time.

Red paper **lanterns** hang everywhere. The lanterns stand for luck and happiness. Photos of past leaders are displayed. People go to concerts and watch fireworks.

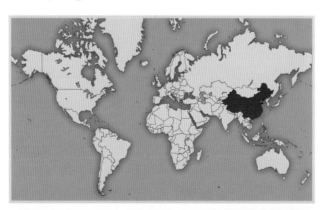

Musicians wearing red and yellow play
drums for National Day in China.

Chapter Seven

Independence Day in Costa Rica

Septtember 15 is Independence Day in Costa Rica. Costa Rica became independent from Spain on that date in 1821. The celebration starts on September 14 at 6:00 p.m. Everyone in the country stops wherever they are to sing the national anthem.

After the song comes the parade of *faroles* (fah-ROH-les). Faroles are lanterns made of cardboard or wood. Each farol has a candle inside. These lanterns remind people of a torch. In 1821, a runner carried a torch across Costa Rica to tell people the country was free. Today, children parade with their faroles through their cities and towns.

The next day, people stay home from work and school. They wear red, white, and blue. These are the colors of Costa Rica's flag. They dance, sing, and play music. People eat tasty food like *arroz con pollo* (ah-ROHZ cown POY-yoh), or "rice with chicken."

Chapter Eight

Fête Nacionale

People in France celebrate becoming a republic on July 14. On July 14, 1789, the French people stormed into a prison called the Bastille. They let out the prisoners. This was the start of the French Revolution. The French overthrew their king in 1789. Now the people rule France instead of a king.

In France, this holiday is called *Fête Nacionale* (FET nah-cee-oh-NAL). People outside of France call it Bastille Day. Soldiers march in a parade in Paris, the capital city. There are fireworks by the Eiffel Tower. There is dancing and music everywhere.

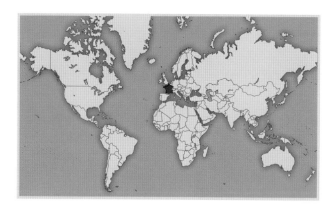

Horses parade through Paris on July 14.

Chapter Nine

Yom Hazikaron and Yom Ha'atzmaut

The country of Israel formed on May 14, 1948. Israelis call their Independence Day *Yom Ha'atzmaut* (yohm ha-AATZ-mah-OOT). Today, they celebrate independence on the fifth day of the Hebrew month *Iyar* (ee-YAHR). This means it falls on a different day of the U.S. calendar every year.

Israel celebrates *Yom Hazikaron* (yohm hah-zih-KAR-own) the day before Yom Ha'atzmaut. Yom Hazikaron is a day to remember people who were killed in wars. People visit graveyards and say prayers.

The Yom Ha'atzmaut celebration starts at sunset the night of Yom Hazikaron. People raise a flag atop a mountain in Jerusalem, the capital city. The president gives a speech. Twelve special people who have helped the country are chosen each year. The 12 people light 12 torches to stand for the 12 ancient tribes of Israel.

Some people celebrate Yom Ha'atzmaut all night. They sing songs and dance together in the streets. The next day, families spend time together.

Chapter Ten

Independence Day in the United States of America

Great Britain created colonies in America beginning around 1600. The United States of America declared it was a free country on July 4, 1776. The country became independent after a long war. Americans gather to celebrate on this day every year.

People from all over the country watch the National Independence Day parade in the capital city of Washington, DC. People dress in red, white, and blue. At night, the National Symphony performs a concert at the Capitol building. Beautiful fireworks finish the night.

People also have parades and fireworks in cities and towns across the country. They have picnics or barbecues. They enjoy a day off work. It is a time to stop and feel pride in their country.

Americans wave flags on the Fourth of July.

Chapter Eleven

Independence Day in Ukraine

Ukraine became an independent country on August 24, 1991. It was ruled by the Union of Soviet Socialist Republics before that. Since 1992, the people have celebrated their country on August 24.

Ukraine celebrates its National Flag Day on August 23. People fly the blue and yellow flag. They are getting ready for Independence Day.

Because their Independence Day is quite new, Ukrainians don't have many **traditions** yet. People stay home from work or school. Some wear traditional clothing. They watch singers in the streets or other shows. Big cities have parades of people from the military. Sometimes there is a big circus in the center of the city. And at night, fireworks light up the sky.

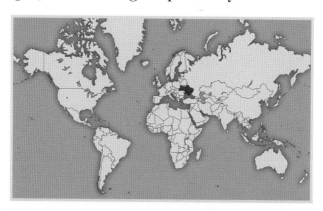

Ukrainians wear traditional decorated shirts on their Independence Day.

Up Close

Most countries have a national anthem or song. People sing the national anthem at special events, like National Days. Canadians sing the national anthem of Canada, "O Canada," in English and in French.

English

O Canada! Our home and native land!
True patriot love in all thy sons command.
With glowing hearts we see thee rise,
The True North strong and free!
From far and wide, O Canada,
We stand on guard for thee.
God keep our land glorious and free!
O Canada, we stand on guard for thee.
O Canada, we stand on guard for thee.

French

Ô Canada! Terre de nos aïeux.
Ton front est ceint de fleurons glorieux.
Car ton bras sait porter l'épée,
Il sait porter la croix.
Ton histoire est une épopée,
Des plus brillants exploits.
Et ta valeur, de foi trempée,
Protégera nos foyers et nos droits,
Protégera nos foyers et nos droits.

Make your own *farol* (lantern), like the children of Costa Rica do!

Materials

old newspaper

small cardboard box (such as a shoe box)

scissors

tape or glue

materials for decorating: markers, paint, colored paper, old buttons, glitter, or other found materials

flashlight or flameless candle

Directions

1. Lay down the newspaper to cover your workspace.
2. Many Costa Rican faroles are in the shape of houses. You can make a house or decide on your own shape.
3. Use scissors and tape or glue to make and attach decorations for your farol. Use markers or paint for color if you like. Be sure to put windows in your lantern so the light will shine through.
4. Put the flashlight or flameless LED candle inside to light it up safely.

Glossary

celebrate (SEL-uh-brate) To celebrate is to observe or take notice of a special day. Many people celebrate National Days.

independence (in-di-PEN-duhns) Independence is freedom from outside control.

lanterns (LAN-turns) Lanterns are small decorative lights. People hang lanterns to celebrate China's National Day.

republic (ri-PUB-lik) A republic is a government in which the people vote for their leaders. The United States is a republic.

traditions (truh-DISH-uns) Traditions are ways of thinking or acting communicated through culture. Many countries have National Day traditions.

Learn More

Books

Heiligman, Deborah. *Celebrate Independence Day*. Washington, DC: National Geographic Children's Books, 2007.

Moehn, Heather. *World Holidays: A Watts Guide for Children*. New York: Franklin Watts, 2000.

Web Sites

Visit our Web site for links about National Day traditions around the world: ***childsworld.com/links***

Note to Parents, Teachers, and Librarians: We routinely verify our Web links to make sure they are safe and active sites. So encourage your readers to check them out!

Index